Published in Moonstone
by Rupa Publications India Pvt. Ltd 2025
7/16, Ansari Road, Daryaganj
New Delhi 110002

Sales centres:
Bengaluru Chennai
Hyderabad Jaipur Kathmandu
Kolkata Mumbai Prayagraj

Copyright © Rupa Publications India Pvt. Ltd 2025

All rights reserved.

No part of this publication may be reproduced, transmitted,
or stored in a retrieval system, in any form or by any means,
electronic, mechanical, photocopying, recording or otherwise,
without the prior permission of the publisher.

P-ISBN: 978-93-6156-520-5
E-ISBN: 978-93-6156-601-1

First impression 2025

10 9 8 7 6 5 4 3 2 1

Printed in India

This book is sold subject to the condition that it shall not,
by way of trade or otherwise, be lent, resold, hired out, or otherwise
circulated, without the publisher's prior consent, in any form of binding
or cover other than that in which it is published.

1. Rearrange the letters in the correct order.

L N E O M

P E P L A

N A A A B N

A E P H C

R E A P

N E O G A R

2. **Match the correct preposition of place to the correct pictures.**

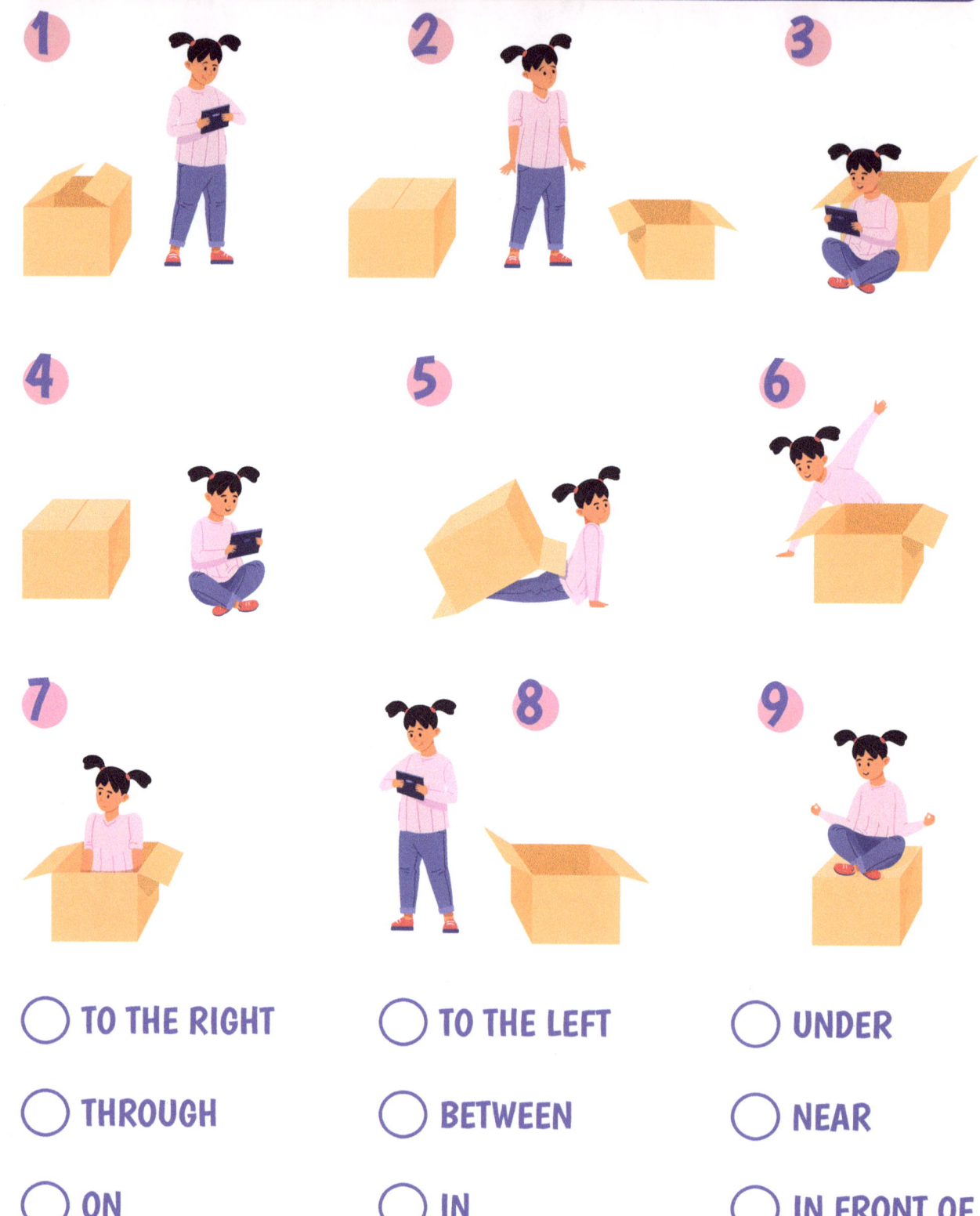

○ TO THE RIGHT   ○ TO THE LEFT   ○ UNDER

○ THROUGH   ○ BETWEEN   ○ NEAR

○ ON   ○ IN   ○ IN FRONT OF

3. Complete the following words.

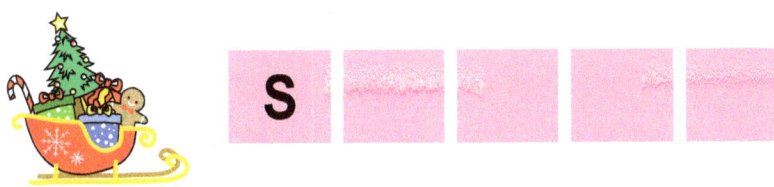 S _ _ _ _ H

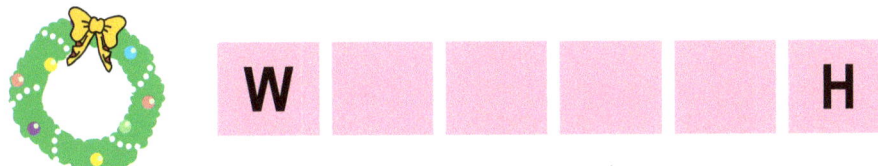 W _ _ _ _ H

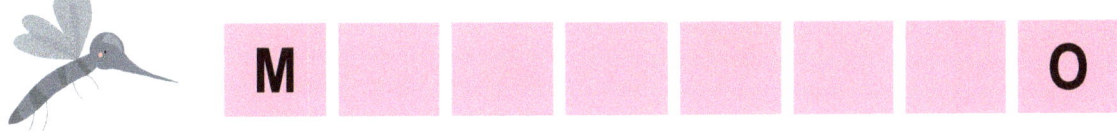 M _ _ _ _ _ _ O

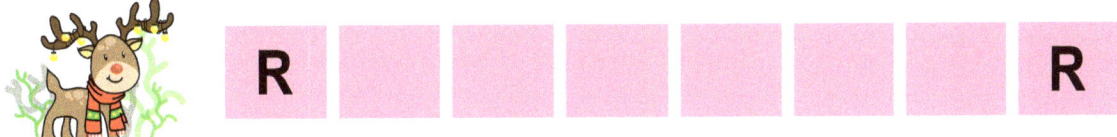 R _ _ _ _ _ _ R

 D _ _ G _ _ _ Y

 P _ _ _ _ T

 S _ _ _ M _ N

4. CVC Words.

CVC words are short, easy-to-read words made up of a consonant, a vowel, and another consonant. These words are great for practising how to sound out letters and blend them together to form words.

 cup
 tap
 dog
 ham
 tag
 kid

 cow
 nut
 sun
 cat
 jam
 tub

Write the correct answer from the CVC wordbank.

B___G	B___T	B___X	C___N
C___P	D___G	F___G	F___N
G___M	J___M	J___R	J___T
L___D	L___G	L___P	M___N
M___P	P___G	P___N	R___M

Word Bank :

LIP   MOP   PAN   BUG   DIG   JAR   PEG
RAM   CUP   LEG   FIG   BAT   FAN   GUM
MEN   BOX   CAN   JET   LID   JAM

5. Fill in the blanks with the correct action verbs.

A verb is a doing word. It tells us what someone or something is doing.

Examples:
Run – I run fast.
Eat – She eats an apple.
So, if it shows action or something happening, it's a verb!

| fly | eat | walk | play | live | swim | love |

I am Fizz. I am a bird but I do not _____.

I am not a fish but I can _____.

I _____ in the cold.

I _____ on my feet.

I _____ fish.

I _____ water.

I _____ with my friends under the water.

6. Circle the correct answer.

BROCCOLI **PAPRIKA**

SANDWICH **CHEETAH**

7. Choose the correct answer.

1. The cat chased the _____ across the garden.
   (a) dog (b) mouse (c) bird

2. To write a letter, you need a pen and _____.
   (a) paper (b) chalk (c) paint

3. During winter, people wear _____ to keep warm.
   (a) sandals (b) shorts (c) coats

4. Birds build their nests in _____.
   (a) water (b) trees (c) caves

5. The teacher asked the students to be _____.
   (a) noisy (b) quiet (c) playful

8. Choose the correct option to describe the picture.

(a) Pair (b) Pear	
(a) Bear (b) Bare	
(a) Flower (b) Flour	
(a) Ring (b) Wring	

9. Unscramble the jumbled sentences.

1. the / morning / rises / sun / in / the
   _____

2. teacher / our / gave / homework / us
   _____

3. a / sings / beautifully / bird
   _____

4. ice cream / loves / my brother / eating
   _____

5. birthday / her / friends / surprised / on / Ella
   _____

10. Find the given words in the word search.

Y	W	A	Z	X	H	D	G	U	F	O
X	E	G	S	T	A	R	J	Z	W	Y
A	A	Y	T	A	G	M	A	B	R	Y
S	R	H	Y	P	Y	G	Y	S	U	N
T	T	B	U	L	P	K	M	L	G	Z
R	H	D	Y	A	L	I	E	N	X	R
O	M	O	O	N	H	B	V	U	T	O
N	X	U	V	E	W	N	Z	P	J	C
A	R	H	J	T	X	R	G	X	J	K
U	N	T	E	L	E	S	C	O	P	E
T	O	G	T	W	X	Y	E	H	D	T

STAR

SUN

ALIEN

ASTRONAUT

MOON

UFO

ROCKET

PLANET

TELESCOPE

EARTH

11. Read the clues carefully and guess the object or thing. Write your answer in the blank space provided.

a. I shine brightly in the sky at night, but I am not the sun. I change my shape from round to thin.

   What am I? _____

b. I have hands but no fingers, I tell you the time day and night.

   What am I? _____

c. I have pages, but I am not a newspaper. Read me to gain knowledge and adventure.

   What am I? _____

d. I have four legs, but I cannot walk. People sit on me to rest or work.

   What am I? _____

12. Write the word that rhymes with the word in bold.

1. The **cat** sat on the m_t.

2. The **dog** jumped over the l_g.

3. The **mouse** ran into the h_ _se.

4. The _____ will shine very **soon**.

5. The **bee** is buzzing near the tr_ _.

6. The _____ goes tick and **tock**.

WORD BANK:

clock

log

tree

mat

moon

house

13. Rearrange them to form a correct sentence.

birthday today It's my. _____

Milk cow The gives us. _____

School go I to every day. _____

Big is elephant The. _____

shines sun The sky the in. _____

14. Match the correct prepositions.

in

to the right of

behind

in front of

on

to the left of

15. Choose the correct word to complete the sentences.

1. We wear a _____ on our head.

2. A _____ has colourful wings.

3. A _____ keeps us warm in winter.

4. The _____ is the king of the jungle.

WORD BANK:

butterfly

lion

hat

jacket

16. Fill in the blank coaches with the correct capital letters.

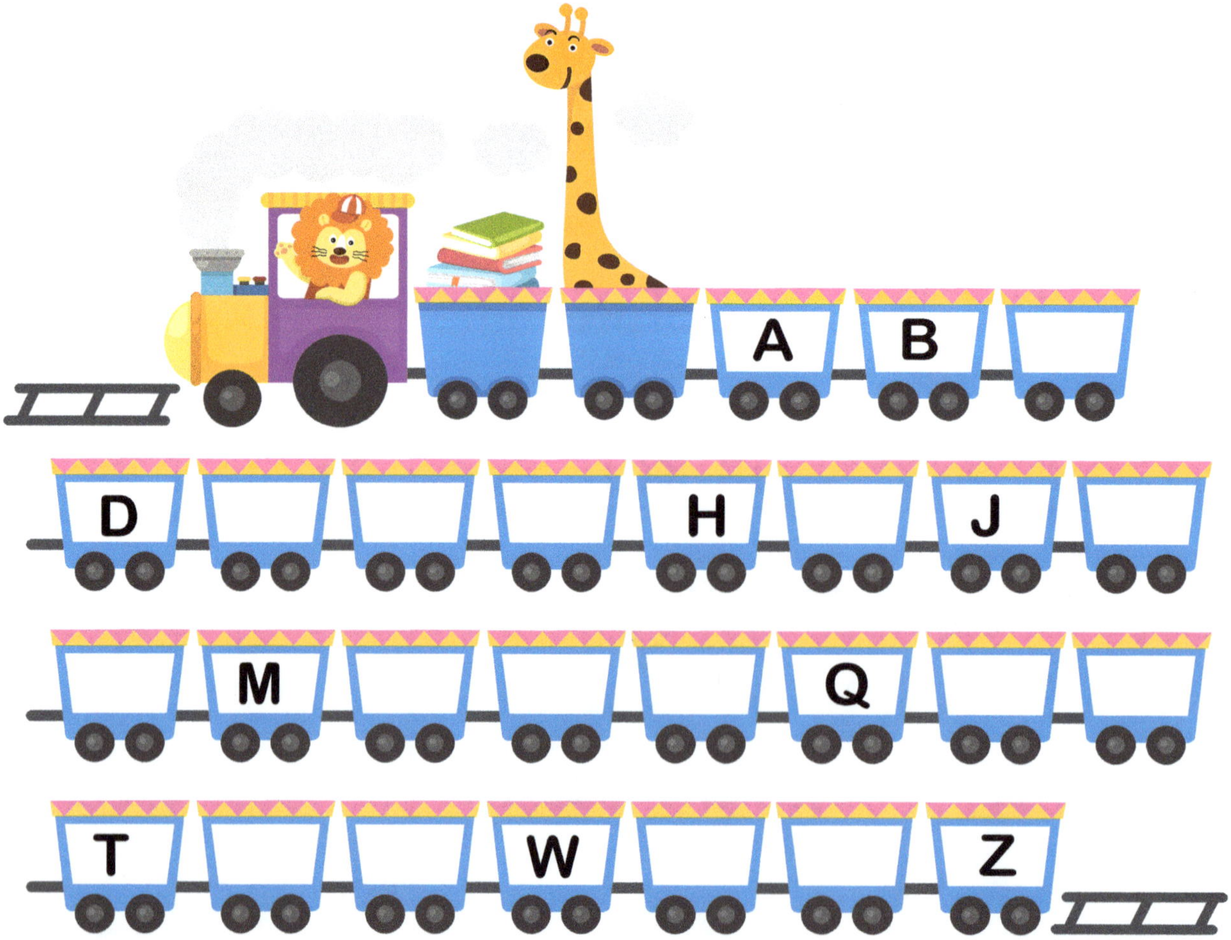

A B ___

D ___ ___ ___ H ___ J ___

___ M ___ ___ ___ Q ___ ___

T ___ ___ W ___ ___ Z

17. Colour accordingly.

18. Colour and answer the question.

What is her name?
_____
_____

19. Find and circle the vocabulary words hidden in the grid.

U	B	L	C	H	I	C	K	E	N
S	U	C	X	B	H	O	R	S	E
U	F	D	U	C	K	A	Y	I	W
G	F	D	P	G	C	F	C	W	P
K	A	O	S	X	O	C	P	M	F
O	L	N	H	G	W	B	X	O	C
P	O	K	E	O	W	C	A	T	G
F	P	E	E	A	U	A	E	Q	I
F	X	Y	P	T	V	Y	I	Y	U
D	O	G	U	T	J	P	I	G	E

**HORSE DUCK DOG COW GOAT SHEEP
CHICKEN DONKEY BUFFALO CAT PIG**

20. Match each picture with its opposite.

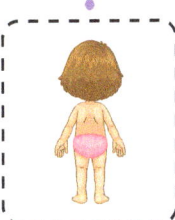    

21. How many, write correctly in words.

How many?

22. Can you correctly identify these cinema-related items from the picture?

....

....

| ticket | film | video | no smoke | prize |
| no camera | director chair | clapperboard | cinema projector | |

23. Mention five after-school activities.

1. _____
2. _____
3. _____
4. _____
5. _____

24. All work and no play? Time for a fun activity game!

How many snakes are there? Write the number in words.

_____

25. Answer them correctly.

What do we need to enter a cinema and watch a movie?
☐ A ticket ☐ A book ☐ A remote control

Which item is used by a director to say 'Action!' before filming a scene?
☐ A popcorn bucket ☐ A clapperboard ☐ A cinema chair

What do we call the machine that projects movies onto the big screen?
☐ A cinema projector ☐ A television ☐ A mobile phone

What should we wear on our eyes to watch a 3D movie?
☐ Sunglasses ☐ 3D glasses ☐ A hat

Which sign tells us that taking photos or videos inside the cinema is not allowed?
☐ No camera sign ☐ Exit sign ☐ Popcorn sign

26. Circle the first letters.

PINE CONE

X V P K
H Z M I
J C Q B
R L S D
G T Y O
W U E N
F A

PINE TREE

S N W A
O C Y B
M P K V
Q H E X
R U G T
Z J D I
L F

REINDEER

A I Y E
B G V T
U C D N
F M O H
S Q X P
W K R J
L Z

RIBBON

H N G Z
R V C A
P F O Y
T I X M
U Q B J
W K L S
E D

27. Match the crayon with the correct picture.

 • •

 • •

 • •

 • •

 • •

 • •

 • •

 • •

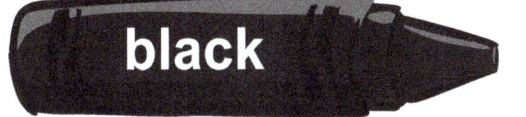 • •

28. Use a / an correctly.

____ owl   ____ umbrella   ____ butterfly

____ ant   ____ robot   ____ flower

____ girl   ____ teacher   ____ car

____ orange   ____ elephant   ____ igloo

29. How many of each item can you find, Miss Detective?

WORD BANK:
Clock Musical note Television Key Umbrella Ruler
Books Plants Hanger Lamp Spoon Apple

30. Circle the correct colour.

✏️	Yellow	Blue	Purple	🍋	Yellow	Green	Pink
🦝	Blue	Grey	Black	🫐	Blue	Purple	White
🍬	Yellow	Pink	Purple	🥕	Yellow	Orange	Purple
🧸	Black	Red	Brown	🥚	Blue	Purple	White
🫛	Blue	Green	Grey	🍐	Blue	Green	Grey
🍎	Yellow	Red	Purple	🐍	Yellow	Green	Blue

31. Colour the rainbow.

Write down the names of all the colours of the rainbow.

1. _____ 2. _____
3. _____ 4. _____
5. _____ 6. _____
7. _____

32. Colour the grid as per the given instructions.

Parts of Speech are the different types of words that make up a sentence. They help us understand how words function in language.

- **Noun** – Colour it **Red**
- **Pronoun** – Colour it **Green**
- **Conjunction** – Colour it **Yellow**
- **Adjective** – Colour it **Violet**

Dog	Since	Bright	He
Car	Although	Happy	Myself
Or	School	Weak	She
If	House	Them	Tall
So	Table	While	Book
Ourselves	Sad	Yet	River

33. Replace the underlined words with their antonyms and rewrite the sentences.

1. The box is **heavy**. _____
2. She looks **happy** today. _____
3. This road is very **narrow**. _____

34. My friend activity corner. Colour and answer.

Ask your friend or sister to fill this up.

NAME

AGE

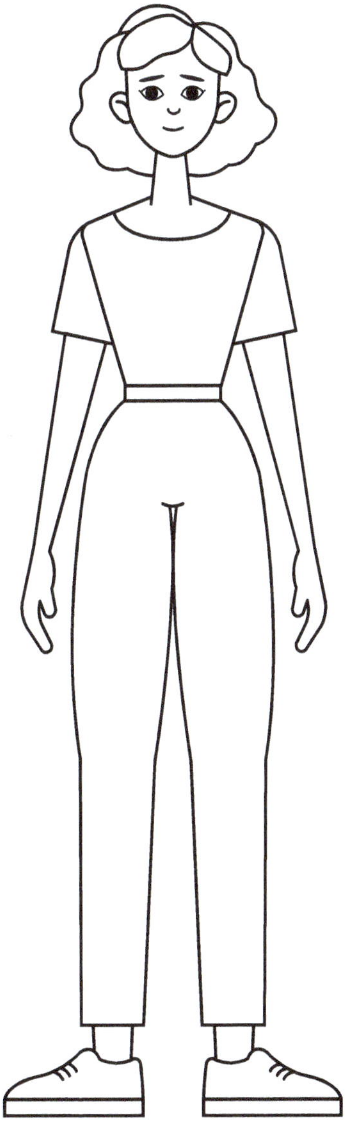

PROFESSION

HOBBIES

DREAMS

QUALITIES

35. Draw a line to match each picture with the correct weather name.

Stormy
Lightning
Sunny
Foggy
Partly cloudy
Hailing
Blizzard
Sleet
Thunderstorm
Rainbow
Windy
Cloudy
Rainy
Snowy

36. Match the following correctly.

TALL LOW SHORT LONG NIGHT DAY SMALL BIG FULL EMPTY

37. Prevention of Coronavirus. Identify the correct instructions with their images.

1. _____
2. _____
3. _____
4. _____

WORD BANK

cleaning hands

cashless transaction

temperature checks

wear masks

38. Choose the correct answer.

1. A train is (slower / faster) than a bicycle.
2. This sofa is (softer / harder) than that chair.
3. The sun is (hotter / colder) than the moon.
4. My shoes are (bigger / smaller) than yours.
5. An elephant is (lighter / heavier) than a dog.

39. Write five sentences about your school.

_____
_____
_____
_____
_____

40. Look at the picture and circle the words that match what you see!

Father	Mother	Boy	Girl	Baby	
Chair	Doll	Books	Lamp	Plants	
Photo Frame	Window	Car	Clock	Dog	
Television	Flower	Carpet	Trees	Cabinet	

41. Arrange the following words in alphabetical order:

- Apple   _____
- Zebra   _____
- Monkey   _____
- Elephant   _____
- Giraffe   _____
- Banana   _____
- Tiger   _____

42. Complete the sentences with "a" or "an".

1. I saw _____ elephant at the zoo.
2. She has _____ orange in her lunchbox.
3. We adopted _____ cute puppy.
4. He is reading _____ interesting book.
5. There is _____ apple on the table.
6. They bought _____ blue car.
7. We saw _____ owl in the tree.
8. I need _____ umbrella because it's raining.
9. She found _____ old coin in the garden.
10. He ate _____ sandwich for lunch.

43. Combine them to form a new word.

1. sun   + shine   = _____
2. play + ground = _____
3. rain + bow   = _____
4. foot + ball   = _____
5. book + shelf   = _____

44. Write a few lines about your time in the park.

45. Complete the word sums to make new words!

1. butter + fly = _____

2. star + fish = _____

3. sea + shell = _____

4. snow + man = _____

46. Sort the Words into the Correct Groups!

ee words : _____

ff words : _____

ll words : _____

oo words : _____

ss words : _____

zz words : _____

Fizz – Cheese – Tree – Gross – Puzzled – Book – Coffee – Moon – Thrill – Stuff
Bell – Buff – Boss – Balloon – Sniff – Middle – Jazz – Green – Class – School
Fizz – Buzz – Miss – Door – Bill – Wheel – Fizzle – Bubble – Giraffe – Glass
Grass – Bee – Glass – Doll – Fizzle – Puzzled – Book – Coffee – Thrill – Cheese

47. Find mistakes and write the correct sentences in the blank spaces.

He have a pet rabbit. _____

They was playing in the park. _____

She don't like eating vegetables. _____

We goes to school every day. _____

48. What is a popular snack people eat while watching a movie?

a) Popcorn   b) Pasta   c) Cake

_____

49. Fill in the blanks with 'a', 'an', or 'the'.

I.   She bought _____ apple from the market.

II.   We saw _____ elephant at the zoo.

III.   He is reading _____ interesting book.

IV.   They live in _____ big house near the park.

V.   I need _____ hour to finish my homework.

VI.   We went to _____ beach last summer.

VII.   There is _____ cat sitting on the roof.

VIII. She drank _____ glass of water.

50. Rewrite the sentences using contractions for the highlighted words.

1. We **do not** like spicy food. _____

2. She **is not** coming to the party. _____

3. They **cannot** find their keys. _____

4. It **will not** rain tomorrow. _____

5. I **am** very tired. _____

51. Match words with their correct pictures.

 • • Rabbit

 • • Duck

 • • Bear

 • • Frog

 • • Hen

 • • Deer

52. Match the type of forces with their images.

  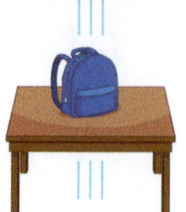 

----------------   ----------------   ----------------   ----------------

----------------   ----------------   ----------------   ----------------

  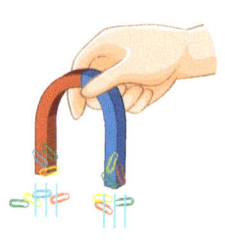  

----------------   ----------------   ----------------   ----------------   ----------------

----------------   ----------------   ----------------   ----------------   ----------------

FRICTION FORCE	APPLIED FORCE	SPRING FORCE
MAGNETIC FORCE	BUOYANT FORCE	ELECTRIC FORCE
DRAG FORCE	NORMAL FORCE	GRAVITY FORCE

53. Read each sentence carefully and circle the adjectives:

I. The beautiful flowers bloomed in the garden.

II. The tall giraffe ate leaves from the tree.

III. She wore a shiny dress to the party.

IV. The angry dog barked loudly.

V. We saw a huge elephant at the zoo.

54. Observe and write the correct answer.

1- It's……………………………………… today.
Put on your coat and scarf.

2- It's……………………………………… today.
Let's go out and have a picnic.

3- It's……………………………………… today.
Don't take your sunglasses.

4- It's……………………………………… today.
Take your umbrella with you.

5- It's……………………………………… today.
Put on a sweater and a jacket.

6- It's……………………………………… today.

55. Write the correct contraction for each set of words.

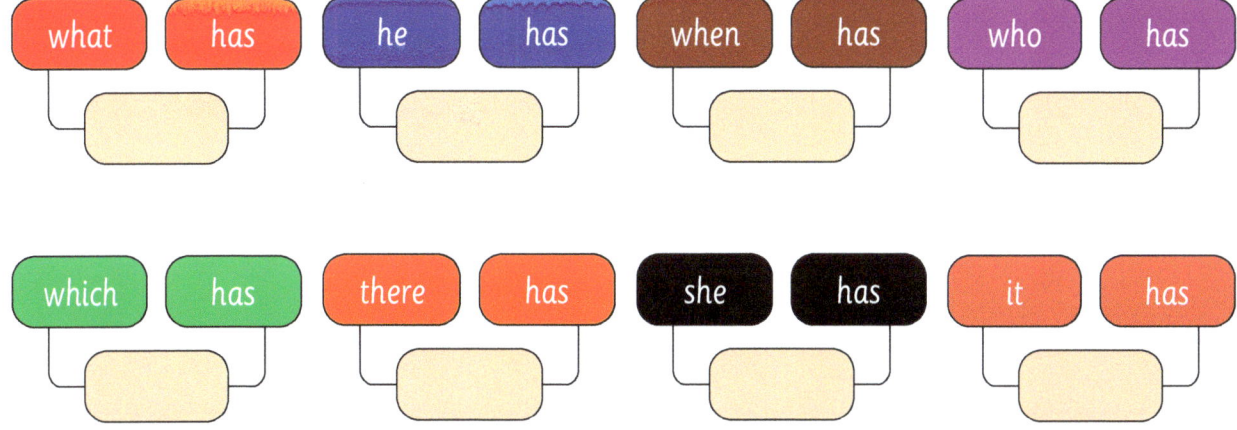

56. Name five clothes that you wear in winter and in summer.

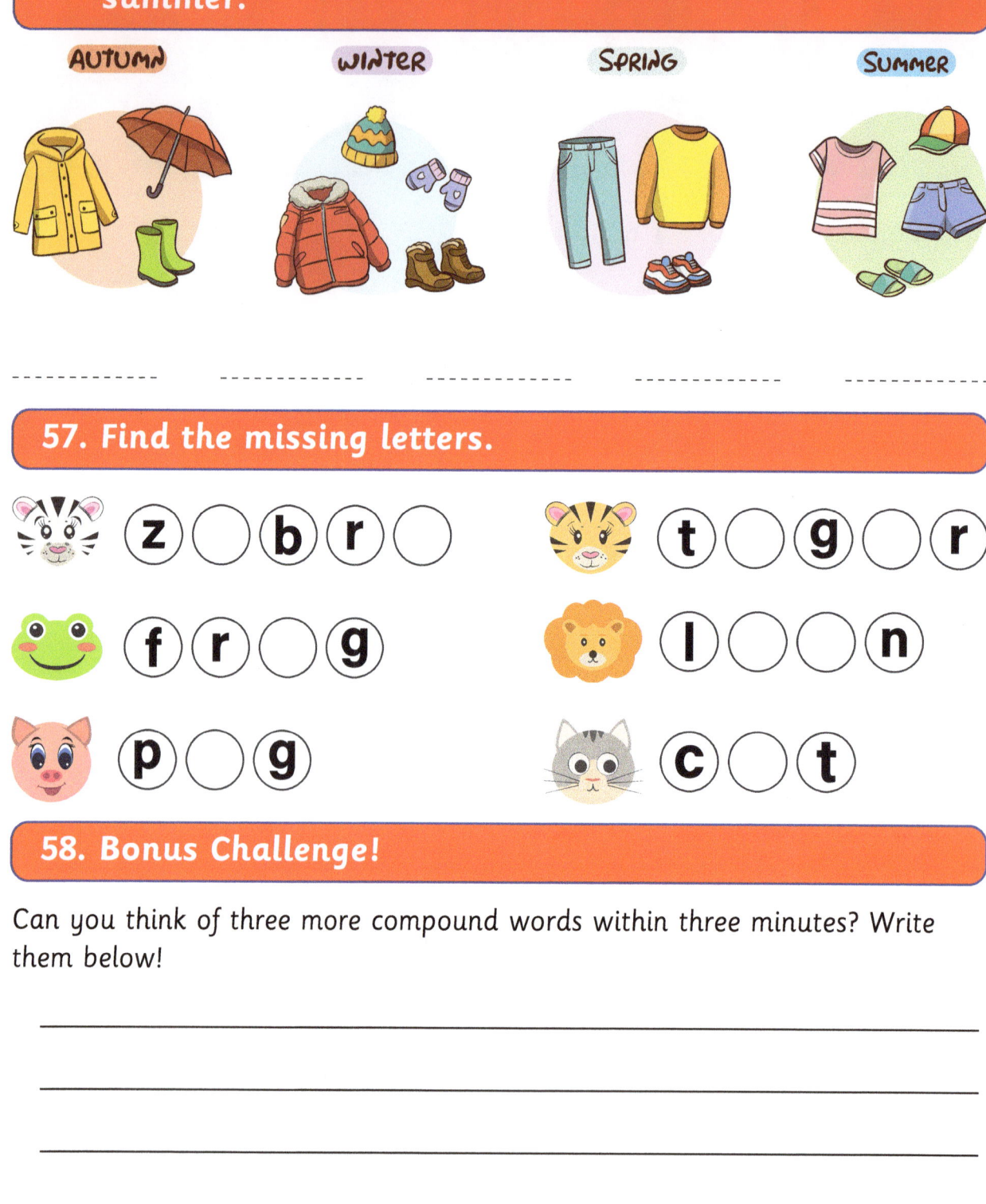

57. Find the missing letters.

z ○ b r ○   t ○ g ○ r
f r ○ g   l ○ ○ n
p ○ ○ g   c ○ t

58. Bonus Challenge!

Can you think of three more compound words within three minutes? Write them below!

_____
_____
_____
_____
_____

59. Silent Letters Dice Game.

Read aloud the given words.

Instructions: Roll a dice. Read a word from the row corresponding to the number you rolled. Each row contains words with a specific silent letter. Practice pronouncing the word, noting the silent letter in it.

Roll Silent Letter Words

Roll				
⚀	lamb	climb	thumb	numb
⚁	knock	knee	knight	know
⚂	honest	hour	heir	herb
⚃	doubt	subtle	debt	receipt
⚄	write	wrong	wrapper	wretch
⚅	gnome	gnash	gnat	sign

Objective: This game helps students recognize and pronounce silent letters in words, reinforcing their phonics skills.

60. A compound word is formed when two words join together to make a new word. Observe carefully and write down the compound words in the space provided.

Example:

Sun + flower = Sunflower

Find the Compound Words!

1. Rain + bow = _____
2. Tooth + brush = _____
3. Foot + ball = _____
4. Butter + fly = _____
5. Snow + man = _____
6. Fire + fly = _____
7. Star + fish = _____

61. Which drink do people often enjoy while watching a movie?

a) Soft drink   b) Tea   c) Soup

_____

62. Arrange the letters and write correctly.

 OMKNYE _____

 TAC _____

 RNAHWLA _____

 FIHS _____

 WLO _____

 RULTTE _____

63. Add an 'e' in the words and see how words change.

I.   Can = _____

II. Tap = _____

III. Kit = _____

IV. Rid = _____

64. Choose 'y' or 'i' to complete the words.

1. H _ p p _ ness _____
2. B a b _ _____
3. C a r r _ _____
4. M e m o r _ _____
5. L a z _ _____
6. F a n c _ _____
7. F r u _ t y _____
8. D a _ l _ _____
9. R a _ n _ _____
10. L u c k _ _____

65. Rewrite the sentence correctly by completing the words.

1. The bab_ is sleeping. _____
2. She has a prett_ dress. _____
3. We saw a luck_ rainbow today. _____
4. His memor_ of that day is very clear. _____
5. The fruit_ cake was delicious! _____

66. Match the idioms to their meanings.

Break the ice. •   • To feel nervous

A piece of cake. •   • To reveal a secret

Spill the beans. •   • To be extremely happy

Once in a blue moon. •   • Feeling unwell

Feeling under the weather. • • Happening very rarely

Over the moon. •   • To start a conversation

67. Circle the verbs with red colour to show the action in each sentence.

1. The dog barks loudly.
2. She runs to school every morning.
3. We played football in the park.
4. He eats an apple for breakfast.
5. The baby sleeps peacefully.

68. Can you write five sentences and circle the verbs?

1. _____
2. _____
3. _____
4. _____
5. _____

69. Fill in the opposites.

1. The suitcase is **light**.
   The suitcase is _____.

2. The children were **quiet** in the library.
   The children were _____ in the library.

3. This road is very **straight**.
   This road is very _____.

4. The question was **difficult**.
   The question was _____.

5. She felt **strong** after eating lunch.
   She felt _____ after eating lunch.

6. The basket is **empty**.
   The basket is _____.

7. The summer air was **hot**.
   The summer air was _____.

8. His clothes were **messy**.
   His clothes were _____.

9. The soldier was **fearless** in battle.
   The soldier was _____ in battle.

10. The book was **boring**.
    The book was _____.

70. Think of five words that contain 'y' or 'i' and write them below:

1. _____
2. _____
3. _____
4. _____
5. _____

71. Choose the correct antonym.

1. The soup was hot.
   a) Warm b) Cold c) Spicy

2. The hallway was dark.
   a) Bright b) Narrow c) Loud

3. The lake is shallow.
   a) Deep b) Wide c) Small

4. The old house was dirty.
   a) Clean b) Empty c) Small

5. The puppy was calm.
   a) Noisy b) Soft c) Happy

72. Write the correct plural form of each word below.

Cat		
Box		
Child		
Leaf		
Woman		

73. Think of five pairs of opposite words and write them below:

- _____ → _____
- _____ → _____
- _____ → _____
- _____ → _____
- _____ → _____

74. Write the opposites of the following.

1. **Heavy** _____
2. **Happy** _____
3. **Narrow** _____
4. **Easy** _____
5. **Weak** _____

75. Match the rhyming words.

Cat	Star
Tree	Night
Car	Tall
Light	Hat
Ball	Bee

76. Choose the correct part of speech for the underlined words in each sentence.

Sentence	Verb	Noun	Adjective
The **dog** barked loudly.			
She **quickly** ran to the door.			
The cake was **delicious**.			
He bought a **new** car.			
We went to the **park** on Sunday.			

77. Look at the object names below and fill in the missing first letter to complete the word.

1. __pple _____

2. __all _____

3. __ouse _____

4. __rain _____

5. __at _____

Colour me.

78. Read the nursery rhyme and fill in the missing letters.

Twinkle, Tw__nkle, Little St__r
How I w__nd__r what y__u are!
Up ab__ve the world so h__gh,
Like a d__ __ __ ond in the sky!

Answer :
Twinkle, Twinkle, Little Star
How I wonder what you are!
Up above the world so high,
Like a diamond in the sky!

Bonus Challenge: Recite the rhyme aloud after filling in the missing letters!

79. Replace the underlined word with its antonym.

The box is **heavy**. _____

She looks **happy** today. _____

This road is very **narrow**. _____

The test was **easy**. _____

He is feeling **weak** after the race. _____

80. Fill in the correct comparative form of the adjective given in brackets.

1. This sofa is _____ than the chair. (comfortable)

2. My suitcase is _____ than yours. (light)

3. Today is _____ than last Monday. (hot)

4. A train is _____ than a bicycle. (slow)

5. This story is _____ than the one I read last month. (exciting)

81. Connect the dots and colour me.

Write down the four things you see here.
_____
_____
_____
_____

82. Look at the picture and fill in the missing letters. Then, put a '/' to separate each syllable in the word.

a _ _ l _	
_ o _ ke _	

83. Think of the first letter of your name. Write two adjectives that start with that letter.

Example:

- If your name is **Sam**, you can write: **Smart, Strong**.

- If your name is **Emily**, you can write: **Energetic, Elegant**.

1. _____

2. _____

84. Can you think of some double-letter words? Say each word loudly.

1. Ha_ _ y

2. Co_ _ ee

3. Bu_ _ er

4. Di_ _ er

5. Sc_ _ ter

Write some double-letter words you can remember.

_____

_____

_____

85. Fill in the blanks with the correct comparative form of the adjective in brackets.

1. This room is _____ than the other one. (clean)

2. My bag is _____ than yours. (heavy)

3. Today is _____ than yesterday. (cold)

4. A cheetah is _____ than a horse. (fast)

5. This book is _____ than the one I read last week. (interesting)

86. Read each sentence carefully, identify the mistakes, and write the correct sentence in the blank provided.

1. The dog chase the cat up the tree.
   Correct sentence: _____

2. It were raining heavily yesterday.
   Correct sentence: _____

3. Me and my friend went to the park.
   Correct sentence: _____

4. She sing beautifully at the concert.
   Correct sentence: _____

87. Write 'a', 'an', or 'the' in the blank spaces to complete each sentence correctly.

1. _____ car is damaged.
2. I found _____ umbrella on the street.
3. She bought _____ apple from the market.
4. We saw _____ elephant at the zoo.
5. He bought _____ interesting book yesterday.

88. Rewrite the sentences using contractions for the highlighted words.

1. **Let us** go for a walk. → _____

2. He **has not** finished his homework. → _____

3. You **should not** talk loudly in the library. → _____

4. We **would not** be late if we leave now. → _____

5. She **had not** seen the movie before. → _____

89. Complete the sentences by writing plurals in the blankets.

1. There are many _____ in the basket. (apple)

2. She bought two _____ from the bakery. (cake)

3. The _____ are playing football. (boy)

4. I saw five _____ in the sky. (bird)

5. The farmer has many _____ on his farm. (cow)

90. Circle the adjectives.

I. He has a soft pillow on his bed.

II. The cold wind made us shiver.

III. The brave firefighter saved the cat.

IV. I love eating sweet apples.

V. The old house creaked in the storm.

91. Find the compound words.

1. **Rain** + **coat** = _____

2. **Cup** + **cake** = _____

3. **Sun** + **flower** = _____

4. **Basket** + **ball** = _____

5. **Butter** + **fly** = _____

92. Circle the verbs (action words) using a red colour pencil.

1. They **wrote** a letter to their friend.
2. I **jumped** over the puddle.
3. The birds **fly** in the sky.
4. She **reads** a storybook before bed.
5. My mother **cooks** tasty food.

93. Which part of speech describes the highlighted words?

1. They **jumped** over the fence. →
   A. Adjective B. Noun C. Verb

2. She sang a **beautiful** song. →
   A. Noun B. Verb C. Adjective

3. We left the house **early**. →
   A. Adverb B. Noun C. Adjective

4. The **team** won the match. →
   A. Noun B. Verb C. Adverb

5. He opened the door **carefully**. →
   A. Adjective B. Noun C. Adverb

94. Colour the rhyming words.

1	CAT	bat	tree
2	BOOK	cook	chair
3	RUN	sun	ball
4	MOUSE	house	door
5	LIGHT	night	kite

95. Fill in the blanks with the correct 'WH' word.

WH words (what, when, where, which, who, why) are used to ask questions.

i. _____ is your name?

ii. _____ are you going on holiday?

iii. _____ is your favourite colour?

iv. _____ took my pencil?

v. _____ is the park located?

vi. _____ is your birthday?

vii. _____ are you feeling sad?

96. Choose the correct nouns.

1. A (car / sing) passed by quickly.
2. The (children / swim) are playing outside.
3. She drank (juice / read) in the morning.
4. He kicked the (ball / sleep) into the net.
5. The (cat / walk) climbed up the tree.
6. We visited the (museum / talk) yesterday.

97. What is your favourite subject and why?

_____
_____
_____
_____
_____

98. Understanding Articles.

Articles are small words used before nouns. They help us know if the noun is general (unspecific) or special (specific).

There are **three** articles in English:

a – used before words starting with consonant sounds.
(a book, a chair)

an – used before nouns starting with vowel sounds (a, e, i, o, u).
(an apple, an elephant)

the – used when we talk about a particular or specific noun.
(the sun, the moon)

Fill in the blanks with the correct article (**a**, **an**, or **the**).

1. I saw _____ elephant at the zoo.

2. She bought _____ banana from the market.

3. _____ sun rises in the east.

4. My mother baked _____ cake yesterday.

5. He is _____ honest boy.

99. Complete the tongue twisters.

Words Box: butter, seashells, woodchuck, pepper, piper

1. She sells _____ by the seashore.

2. Peter _____ picked a peck of pickled _____.

3. How much wood would a _____ chuck, if a woodchuck could chuck wood?

4. Betty bought a bit of _____.

100. Read the nouns below. Write each one in the correct column based on its gender.

Nouns:
uncle, woman, king, queen, boy, aunt, man, niece, girl, nephew

Masculine Gender	Feminine Gender
_____	_____
_____	_____
_____	_____
_____	_____
_____	_____

101. Arrange the words in alphabetical order.

1. **Sun**, **Moon**, **Earth**, **Star**

   (_____) (_____) (_____) (_____)

2. **Tiger**, **Bear**, **Lion**, **Elephant**

   (_____) (_____) (_____) (_____)

3. **Book**, **Pencil**, **Desk**, **Chair**

   (_____) (_____) (_____) (_____)

4. **Red**, **Blue**, **Green**, **Yellow**

   (_____) (_____) (_____) (_____)

5. **Carrot**, **Potato**, **Tomato**, **Apple**

   (_____) (_____) (_____) (_____)

102. Write three singular words you can think of. Then write their plural forms.

103. Choose and circle the correct meaning from the given options.

1. **Tiny** A. Very big B. Very small C. Very hot
2. **Brave** A. Happy B. Afraid C. Courageous
3. **Delicious** A. Tasty B. Dirty C. Bitter
4. **Swift** A. Fast B. Slow C. Quiet
5. **Wealthy** A. Sick B. Rich C. Poor

104. Complete the sentence using the correct options.

- The dog wagged its _____. (tale, tail)
- The sun will _____ in the east. (rise, rice)
- This is a _____ story. (true, threw)
- My mother _____ a cake for me. (maid, made)
- She will _____ a new dress today. (buy, by)

105. Colour all the uppercase C in red and lowercase c letters in blue colours.

B	a	C	e	D	K	c	b
D	c	W	b	C	A	i	S
F	P	g	F	h	J	O	c
M	h	C	i	B	b	T	h

106. Write the plurals of the following words.

1. **Bus** _____

2. **Mouse** _____

3. **Potato** _____

4. **Foot** _____

5. **Tooth** _____

107. Write the opposites of the following.

1. **Full** _____

2. **Cold** _____

3. **Clean** _____

4. **Brave** _____

5. **Interesting** _____

108. Write the missing beginning letter of each object.

1. __lower _____

2. __un _____

3. __arrot _____

4. __ish _____

5. __og _____

109. Replace the underlined words with their antonyms.

1. The tea is **hot**.   The tea is _____.

2. Her hair is **long**.   Her hair is _____.

3. The book was **boring**.   The book was _____.

4. This box is **light**.   This box is _____.

5. The classroom is **quiet**. The classroom is _____.

110. Fill in the blanks with the correct comparative form of the adjective.

1. The black shoes are _____ than the brown ones. (cheap)
2. My grandmother is _____ than my uncle. (old)
3. The tower is _____ than the building. (tall)
4. A tiger is _____ than a cat. (dangerous)
5. My cousin's hair is _____ than mine. (short)

111. Fill in each blank with the correct double letters.

1. Mu _ _ in
2. Ki _ _ en
3. Pu _ _ le
4. Ba _ _ oon
5. Le _ _ er
6. Bu _ _ erfly
7. Su _ _ er
8. Po _ _ y
9. P _ _ dle
10. Li _ _ le
11. Sco _ _ er
12. A _ _ le
13. Co _ _ ee
14. Be _ _ er
15. Cu _ _ le

| Muffin | Kitten | Puzzle | Balloon | Letter | Better | Summer | Poppy |
| Happy | Little | Coffee | Butterfly | Poodle | Apple | Scooter | Cuddle |

112. Write the correct option clearly.

1. I _____ some bread. (have got / has got)
2. The dog _____ barking loudly. (is / am / are)
3. They _____ playing football. (is / am / are)
4. She _____ long hair. (have got / has got)

113. Draw a line to match each double letter word with its correct meaning.

Word	Meaning
Coffee •	• A small baked cake
Letter •	• A two-wheeled vehicle
Kitten •	• A baby cat
Muffin •	• A message written on paper
Scooter •	• A hot drink made from beans

114. Read the story and answer the questions.

Tom and Anna are brother and sister. They went to the park on Sunday. It was sunny outside, and they played football. Tom kicked the ball, and Anna caught it. Later, they sat under a big tree and ate sandwiches. They had a lovely time at the park.

1. Who went to the park?
2. On which day did they go to the park?
3. How was the weather outside?
4. What did they play at the park?
5. Where did Tom and Anna sit to eat their sandwiches?

Answers:

1. _____
2. _____
3. _____
4. _____
5. _____

115. Circle the words that begin with a consonant sound.

(Remember: consonants are all letters except **a, e, i, o, u**.)

1. apple, **ball**, orange, **cat**
2. umbrella, **dog**, ice, **frog**
3. elephant, **goat**, **hat**, ant
4. egg, **jug**, **kite**, owl
5. igloo, **lion**, **monkey**, apricot
6. **tree**, ear, onion, **pen**
7. **car**, apple, umbrella, **rabbit**
8. octopus, **snake**, **table**, egg

116. Colour the flower and name it. Now, write 8 flower names you can remember.

1. _____
2. _____
3. _____
4. _____
5. _____
6. _____
7. _____
8. _____

_____

117. Read each sentence carefully and circle the nouns.

1. The cat is sleeping on the bed.
2. She bought apples from the market.

118. Fill the Blanks with "to", "too", or "two".

1. I have _____ apples in my lunchbox.
2. She went _____ the store.
3. It's _____ cold outside.
4. Can you come _____ my party?
5. My little sister is _____ years old.
6. This bag is _____ heavy for me.
7. I would like _____ have some ice cream.
8. We saw _____ birds on the tree.
9. It's late; I need _____ go home now.
10. My friend is coming _____.

119. Guess the word.

- You can use this to write.   Answer: _____
- You can read this.   Answer: _____
- It tells the time.   Answer: _____

120. Write down two words that rhyme with each word given below.

1. **Rain** _____
11. **Door** _____

121. Write five words with a vowel (a, e, i, o, u) in the middle.

1. _____
2. _____
3. _____
4. _____
5. _____

122. Write the missing beginning letter to complete it correctly.

____ at		____ um	
____ og		____ all	
____ ish		____ an	

123. Understanding sound blends.

Sound blends are two or three consonants joined together, where each consonant's sound can still be heard clearly. Blends can appear at the **beginning** or at the **end** of a word.

Examples of blends:
- **Beginning blends:**
  br in **br**own, **cl** in **cl**ock, **st** in **st**ar

- **Ending blends:**
  mp in la**mp**, **nd** in ha**nd**, **st** in be**st**

Circle the consonant blends in each word below.

1. Flower   2. Clock   3. Hand   4. Bread   5. Lamp
6. Star   7. Desk   8. Frog   9. Nest   10. Tree

124. Rearrange the sentences below in the correct order.

- He ran fast to catch it.

- Suddenly, his hat flew off.

- John was walking to school.

- He put the hat back on his head and continued walking.

Correct Order:

1. _____

2. _____

3. _____

4. _____

125. Choose the correct option from the brackets to complete each sentence.

1. She _____ to school every day. (go / goes)
2. The cats _____ playing outside. (is / are)
3. I _____ breakfast this morning. (eat / ate)
4. My sister _____ two apples yesterday. (buy / bought)
5. He _____ very fast. (run / runs)

126. Colour the words in each set that rhyme with each other.

CAT:	hat	sun
FISH:	dish	shoe
CUP:	pup	book
BED:	red	car
NIGHT:	light	ball

127. Place each noun in the correct column: Name, Place, Thing, or Animal.

Words Box:

school   lion   chair   India   John   pencil,
park   cat   hospital   apple   teacher   London

Name	Place	Thing	Animal

128. Understanding Syllables.

A syllable is a part of a word containing one vowel sound. The number of syllables a word has depends on how many vowel sounds you can hear when you say the word aloud.

Example:
- **Cat** has 1 syllable: (cat)
- **Ap-ple** has 2 syllables (ap-ple).
- **Banana** has 3 syllables (ba-na-na).

Write the number of syllables it has in the blank provided.

1. Apple   _____
2. Elephant   _____
3. Balloon   _____
4. Cat   _____
5. Butterfly   _____

129. Match the Idioms with their meanings.

Break the ice	Feeling sick or unwell.
Hit the nail on the head	Something very easy to do.
Under the weather	To describe exactly what is causing a situation or problem.
Spill the beans	To reveal a secret.
A piece of cake	To start a conversation and make people feel comfortable.

130. Tick (✓) the correct word that best matches the description.

1. A person who treats sick people.
   ☐ Carpenter   ☐ Mechanic   ☐ Doctor   ☐ Farmer

2. A place where students study.
   ☐ Hospital   ☐ Library   ☐ School   ☐ Market

3. A person who fixes pipes and taps.
   ☐ Electrician   ☐ Plumber   ☐ Chef   ☐ Barber

4. The opposite of happy.
   ☐ Sad   ☐ Angry   ☐ Excited   ☐ Joyful

131. a. It shines in the sky at night.

Answer: _____

132. b. You use this to drink water.

Answer: _____

133. Look at the pictures and write the new word.

(These are **compound words**.)

 +  = _____

 +  = _____

 +  = _____

 +  = _____

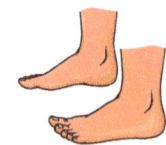 +  = _____

134. Look around your room and find objects that match the colours listed below.

Draw one of the colourful objects you have found and write its name.

135. Match the pictures with the words that rhyme.

🐱	• — •	Bat
☀️	• — •	Run
🌳	• — •	Bee
🎩	• — •	Mat
🏐	• — •	Tall
⭐	• — •	Car
🦆	• — •	Truck
🪑	• — •	Bear

136. Fill in the blanks with suitable words from the box.

Word Box: brave, swim, beach, arms, legs, lunch

Liam is a _____ boy. He loves to _____ in the sea. Every weekend, he goes to the _____ with his family. He moves his _____ and kicks his _____ in the water. After playing, he sits with his parents and eats his _____ under the sun.

137. Fill in the blanks with the most suitable adverbs from the box.

Word Box: softly, beautifully, late, quickly, carefully, loudly

1. Malfoy plays the guitar _____.
2. She arrived _____ for the meeting.
3. The dog barked _____ at the stranger.
4. Xena always speaks _____.
5. He completed his homework _____.
6. She walked _____ on the slippery floor.

138. Read the paragraph below and underline all the adverbs.

Lucy woke up early and got dressed quickly. She walked happily to school, but the wind blew strongly. The teacher spoke calmly while the students listened carefully. After the lesson, they played joyfully in the playground.

139. Match each verb with the most suitable adverb from the box.

Word Box: quickly, softly, loudly, carefully, happily, lazily

Verb		Adverb
Speak	• •	_____
Run	• •	_____
Sing	• •	_____
Write	• •	_____
Laugh	• •	_____
Walk	• •	_____

140. Use the adverbs from the word box to write your own sentences.

Word Box: cheerfully, silently, angrily, brightly, politely, suddenly

1. _____
2. _____
3. _____
4. _____
5. _____

141. Choose the correct adverb from the options in brackets.

1. He completed his homework _____. (quickly / loudly / sadly)
2. The baby slept _____. (softly / rudely / brightly)
3. She greeted the teacher _____. (politely / carelessly / angrily)
4. He waited _____ for the bus to arrive. (patiently / foolishly / loudly)
5. The sun shone _____ in the sky. (brightly / rudely / happily)

142. Identify the adverb and write them down below:

early   quickly   happily   strongly   calmly   carefully   joyfully

- _____
- _____

143. Fill in the missing blends to complete each word and sentence.

1. Sam _ _ **imbs** the tree quickly.
2. The snake _ _ **ides** on the ground.
3. The baby sleeps in a _ _ **ib**.
4. The farmer keeps cows in a _ _ _ **n**.

WORD BANK
Crib
Barn
Slides
Climbs

144. Use the words from the word box to complete the story.

Word Box: cousin's   passion   enjoy   café   title   cook

Hi, my _____ is Ria. I am a _____. I _____ making all kinds of pasta, _____, and sandwiches. My personal _____ is the cheesy lasagna. I work in my _____ café.

145. What does "Plural" mean?

Plurals are words that **denote more than one** of something. For example:

1. **One** cat → **Many** cats   2. **One** book → **Many** books

Write the plural form of each word in the blank space provided.

Ball _____	
Tomato _____	
Child _____	
Doll _____	
Tree _____	

146. Complete the sentences by writing plurals.

1. My mother has two _____. (watch)

2. There are many _____ in the park. (tree)

3. The classroom has many _____. (chair)

4. We ate three _____ today. (sandwich)

5. There are seven _____ swimming in the pond. (duck)

6. She loves to read _____. (book)

147. Draw a line between the two words that make up a new word (compound word).

Sun	•	•	Room	_____
Tooth	•	•	Brush	_____
Rain	•	•	Man	_____
Note	•	•	Ball	_____
Foot	•	•	Book	_____
Snow	•	•	Ball	_____
Butter	•	•	Cake	_____
Bed	•	•	Coat	_____
Pan	•	•	Shine	_____
Basket	•	•	Fly	_____

148. Look at each picture and circle the correct word.

1. The boy is wearing his new – **shoe / shoes**

2. The children are playing with – **ball / balls**

3. She packed her – **bag / bags** for school.

4. The cat is chasing the – **mouse / mice**

149. Fill in the blanks with the correct comparative form of the adjective in brackets.

1. The blue dress is _____ than the red one. (expensive)
2. My grandfather is _____ than my father. (old)
3. The mountain is _____ than the hill. (high)
4. A lion is _____ than a rabbit. (strong)
5. My sister's hair is _____ than mine. (long)

150. Fill in the blanks with 'a', 'an', or 'the'.

1. _____ sun shines brightly in the sky.
2. She lives in _____ big house near the park.
3. _____ lion is the king of the jungle.
4. Can you give me _____ pencil, please?
5. She ate _____ orange after dinner.

151. Write five nouns that start with the letter "T".

1. _____
2. _____
3. _____
4. _____
5. _____

152. What is your pronoun? Write here.

_____
_____

153. Write five flowers that are white in colour.

1. _____
2. _____
3. _____
4. _____
5. _____

154. Find the compound words!

1. **Tooth** + **brush** = _____
2. **Snow** + **man** = _____
3. **Moon** + **light** = _____
4. **Bed** + **room** = _____
5. **Foot** + **ball** = _____

155. Circle the verbs with red colour to show the action in each sentence.

1. The dog runs in the garden.

2. He kicks the football into the goal.

3. We swim in the pool.

4. She sings beautifully on stage.

5. The boy paints a lovely picture.

156. Colour the rhyming words.

BEE	tree	shoe
CAR	star	cow
FISH	dish	duck
CAKE	bake	lake
SPOON	moon	balloon

157. Circle or underline the correct noun to complete the sentence.

1. I eat an (apple / jump) every day.

2. The (dog / run) is barking loudly.

3. She wrote with a (pencil / beautiful).

4. The (flower / happy) smells nice.

5. The (teacher / play) reads a story to the class.

158. Fill in the blanks with the correct article (a, an, or the).

1. Please open _____ window.

2. She has _____ umbrella.

3. This is _____ interesting story.

4. _____ moon shines at night.

5. He bought _____ new bicycle.

159. Choose and circle the correct meaning from the given options.

1. **Ancient**   A. Very new   B. Very old   C. Very clean

2. **Silent**   A. Noisy   B. Quiet   C. Sad

3. **Huge**   A. Tiny   B. Large   C. Pretty

4. **Polite**   A. Rude   B. Angry   C. Well-mannered

5. **Cheerful**   A. Sad   B. Happy   C. Angry

160. Complete the sentence using the correct options.

- She loves to eat _____ for breakfast. (serial, cereal)

- He couldn't _____ the bell ringing. (hear, here)

- I _____ a blue shirt yesterday. (wore, war)

- Please _____ quietly in the library. (be, bee)

161. Read each sentence carefully and circle the nouns.

1. My brother plays football.

2. The book is on the table.

3. Birds fly in the sky.

4. The girl is riding her bicycle.

162. Rearrange the jumbled sentences.

Passage

- She paid the shopkeeper and went home happily.
- Sara wanted a new dress.
- She tried on many dresses.
- Finally, she found one that she liked.

Correct Order:

1. _____
2. _____
3. _____
4. _____

163. Complete the sentences using the correct options.

1. The bird _____ singing sweetly. (is / am)

2. My mother _____ cooking now. (are / is)

3. We _____ going to the park. (are / is)

4. She _____ her homework daily. (do / does)

5. They _____ football last evening. (play / played)

164. Look at the pictures and circle the correct answer.

1. He is holding a – **book / books**

2. They are sitting on – **bench / benches**

3. My sister has long – **scarf / scarves**

4. The baby is playing with – **toy / toys**

5. We saw many – **bird / birds** in the park.

165. Complete the words with missing blends.

1. The children played near the _ _ **ee**.

2. The princess lived in a _ **astle**.

3. Dad fixed the broken _ **ate**.

4. The ship sails across the _ _ **ean**.

5. The birds _ _ **y** in the sky.

(**word bank:** gate castle ocean tree fly)

166. Bonus Challenge:

Think of three more words that contain **blends** (e.g., **bl, dr, sp, br, tr**) and write them below:

1. _____

2. _____

3. _____

167. Write the number of syllables it has in the blank provided.

1. Apple _____ syllable(s)

2. Elephant _____ syllable(s)

3. Balloon _____ syllable(s)

4. Cat _____ syllable(s)

5. Butterfly _____ syllables

168. Write the plural form of each word in the blank space provided.

1. **Box** _____

2. **Child** _____

3. **Tomato** _____

4. **Man** _____

5. **Leaf** _____

169. Use the correct action verbs.

....

Word Box: Standing   Sitting   Painting   Dancing

170. Can you identify the colours.

....

Word Box: Blue   Red   Yellow   Pink

171. Identify the professions.

....

Word Box: Astronaut   Painter   Car racer   Singer   Professor

172. Please colour me!

Can you think of a name for me?
_____

173. Fill in the blanks.

1. The children are exploring _____ (nature/city).

2. One boy is using a _____ (binocular/microscope) to look at the sky.

3. The girl with the red backpack is _____ (drawing/writing).

4. There is a _____ (dog/cat) playing in the grass.

5. The children seem to be having a _____ (boring/fun) time.

6. The children are wearing _____ (school uniforms/casual clothes).

7. The plants in the forest are _____ (dry/green).

8. One child is using a _____ (magnifying glass/telescope) to observe insects.

174. Observe the picture very carefully and answer the questions.

1. The people in the picture are _____ (dancing/sleeping).

2. They all look _____ (sad/happy).

3. Some people are wearing _____ (skirts/hats).

4. The background is _____ (white/blue).

5. They are all moving their _____ (arms/feet).

175. Draw a picture of yourself dancing and colour it.

176. Observe the picture very carefully and match each emotion with the correct description.

Emotion	Description
Happy	A. Feeling nervous or uneasy.
Angry	B. Feeling very tired after doing something.
Curious	C. Feeling joy or excitement.
Confused	D. Feeling unsure or not understanding something.
Scared	E. Feeling like you want to explore or learn new things.
Crying	F. Feeling upset and tears come out of your eyes.
Sad	G. Feeling mad or frustrated.
Tired	H. Feeling worried or scared about something.
Anxious	I. Feeling unhappy or lonely.

SCARED

CURIOUS

SAD

CONFUSED

CRY

ANGRY

HAPPY

ANXIOUS

TIRED

177. Think and answer.

1. Do you like to dance? Why or why not?
   _____

2. Have you ever performed a dance in school? Describe your experience.
   _____

3. What is your favourite type of dance?
   _____

178. Unscramble the jumbled sentences.

1. the / swims / in / pond / duck / the
   _____

2. his / carefully / wrote / essay / Jack
   _____

179. Fill in the blanks.

1. When I get a new toy, I feel _____.

2. If I lose my favourite book, I will feel _____.

3. If I don't understand my homework, I will feel _____.

4. When my best friend makes me laugh, I feel _____.

5. If I hear a loud noise at night, I will feel _____.

180. Draw a picture of yourself showing any one of the emotions in the worksheet.

181. Think and answer.

1. What makes you feel happy?

   _____

2. What do you do when you feel sad?

   _____

3. Describe a time when you felt curious about something.

   _____

   _____

182. Choose the correct word – "to", "too", or "two"

1. I want _____ read a new book.

2. She has _____ pets at home.

3. This coffee is _____ hot to drink.

4. We are going _____ the beach tomorrow.

5. He was feeling sick, so he stayed home _____.

6. The teacher gave us _____ assignments for the weekend.

7. I need _____ buy some groceries after work.

8. There are _____ cakes left on the plate.

9. She walked _____ school with her best friend.

10. This song is _____ loud, can you turn it down?

183. Find and underline the correct word in each sentence below:

a) We are going (to/too/two) the cinema.

b) The dress is (to/too/two) small for me.

c) She ate (to/too/two) slices of cake.

184. Fill in the missing beginning letter for each word to complete the name of the object.

1. __og _____

2. __lower _____

3. __un _____

4. __arrot _____

5. __ish _____

185. Draw a picture of one of the words mentioned in question 187 and colour it.

186. Colour the flower and the bee by alphabet.

187. Match words with the correct pictures.

188. **Read the sentence and then colour the object it mentions in the picture.**

I SEE A MUSHROOM

I SEE A SHEEP

I SEE A DUCK

I SEE A CRAB

I SEE A FLOWER

I SEE A ROCKET

I SEE A FISH

I SEE A WATERMELON

189. Find the missing letter.

(Q) (O) (P)

_____ nion

(N) (Y) (U)

_____ ail

(W) (M) (V)

_____ ilk

(D) (P) (Z)

_____ izza

190. Match each picture with their matching colours.

191. Write the correct numbers of body parts.

1. Antennae
2. Head
3. Eye
4. wings
5. sting
6. Body
7. leg

192. Fill in the missing letters.

193. Identify the body parts.

Word Bank: Eye Nose Head Ear Teeth Mouth Arm Leg Foot Hand

194. Look at the picture carefully and answer the following questions.

1. The children are in a _____ (garden/city).

2. They are looking at a _____ (bird/ladybug).

3. The boy is holding a _____ (notebook/ball).

4. The girl's bag is _____ (red/blue).

5. The sky has _____ (clouds/stars) in it.

195. Count and write the numbers in words.

| bird | worm | owl | pumpkin | duck |

196. Fill in the correct number in front of the pictures.

1. horse
2. cow
3. dog
4. monkey
5. sheep
6. rabbit
7. goose
8. cat
9. zebra
10. hen

197. Look at the picture carefully and complete the activities below.

1. How many children are in the picture? _____
2. What is behind the children? _____
3. Are the children holding hands? (Yes/No) _____

198. Look at the picture carefully and complete the activities below.

1. How many balloons are floating in the air? _____
2. What colours are the balloons?_____
3. The girl is blowing a _____ (balloon/ball).
4. The balloons are _____ (square/round) in shape.
5. There are _____ (two/three) balloons on the table.
6. The girl has a _____ (red/yellow) bow in her hair.
7. The balloons are floating _____ (on/in) the air.

199. REVISION. Fill in the missing letters.

 p ◯ g    c ◯ t

 f r ◯ g    l ◯ ◯ n

 z ◯ b r ◯    t ◯ g ◯ r

200. Write the synonyms of the given words.

- Sad — _____
- Fast — _____
- Slow — _____
- Big — _____
- Small — _____
- Happy — _____
- Angry — _____
- Cold — _____
- Hot — _____
- Beautiful — _____
- Easy — _____
- Hard — _____
- Funny — _____
- Smart — _____
- Tired — _____

Word Bank

Unhappy
Quick
Lazy
Large
Tiny
Chilly
Clever
Difficult
Mad
Pretty
Exhausted
Hilarious
Simple
Joyful
Warm

201. Draw three balloons in your favourite colours and then write the names of the colours used.

www.ingramcontent.com/pod-product-compliance
Lightning Source LLC
Chambersburg PA
CBHW061116170426
43198CB00026B/2997